JUST IN TIME!

PRAYERS FOR LENT AND HOLY WEEK

JUST IN TIME!

PRAYERS FOR LENT AND HOLY WEEK

Edited by
David Neil Mosser Sr.
with
Estee Carel Valendy

Abingdon Press
Nashville

JUST IN TIME!
PRAYERS FOR LENT AND HOLY WEEK

Copyright © 2010 by Abingdon Press

All rights reserved.

This book is printed on acid-free paper.

Library of Congress Cataloging-in-Publication Data

Prayers for Lent and Holy Week / edited by David Neil Mosser Sr. ; with Estee Carel Valendy.
    p.   cm.—(Just in time!)
    Includes bibliographical references and index.
    ISBN 978-1-4267-1031-5 (binding: pbk. : alk. paper)
1. Lent—Prayers and devotions. 2. Holy Week—Prayers and devotions. I. Mosser, David, 1952- II. Valendy, Estee Carel.
    BV85.P73 2010
    242'.34—dc22

                               2010042939

10 11 12 13 14 15 16 17 18 19—10 9 8 7 6 5 4 3 2 1

MANUFACTURED IN THE UNITED STATES OF AMERICA

With loving-kindness to the young ministers of the

Central Texas Annual Conference of The United

Methodist Church and a leader who inspires them:

Bishop John Michael Lowry

CONTENTS

INTRODUCTION

Simply put, this is chiefly a book of liturgical prayers for use in public worship by the community of faith. These prayers are for occasions of the Christian year when the church journeys thorough the darkest moments of the Jesus story as Jesus is on his way to the cross. These prayers not only prepare for the "shadow of death" times but also help believers anticipate the joy of Easter's promise. Lent begins on Ash Wednesday. For most churches the Lenten observance ends on Good Friday, although technically it extends through the Easter vigil or in some traditions Holy Saturday. In our worship experiences we reflect on the profundity of Jesus' passion and death, and anticipate his decisive resurrection. As we ponder these aspects of Jesus' humanity, we therefore consider our humanity too. Consequently Lent is the time of the liturgical year when Christians explore together what it means to be fully human.

As we observe human life reflected in modern culture, many individuals appear increasingly more disconnected and more privatized. If this is true, then public worship also may be on the wane, as are other modes of long-established community behavior. Perhaps an element of this individualistic tendency pertains to personal computers and cell phones that no doubt contribute to introverted behaviors not common thirty years ago. In other words, people today have multiple options from which to choose in order to disengage from community life.

Further, in terms of faith community, we regularly hear people suggest that they are "spiritual" but not "religious." Despite a spate of self-medicating spirituality that has run amok in our culture, there is a faithful and tradition-observing segment of our church culture that still believes not only in private but also deliberate public prayer. Abingdon Press's intention for this specific volume in the Just in Time! series is to provide resources for communal prayer for those who lead and participate in public worship during Lent and Holy Week. These forty days tend to be when the church is at its most self-reflective best.

In our fast-paced world most of us know what it is like to have too much to do and seemingly too little time in which to do it. It is often easy enough for us to let the most momentous parts of life slip by the wayside. Our fervent mantra is *mañana,* or tomorrow, as we who live near the United States' southern border are fond of saying. We will attend to these weighty matters and events tomorrow, or perhaps the day after that. But during the season of Lent we humans face questions about life and death that, in many respects, we cannot put off. Lent questions are not simply questions asked during Lent. Rather we ask Lent-type questions at the scene of an automobile accident, in the parlor of a funeral home, in an ambulance en route to the emergency room, or at the bedside of a stricken patient. These questions are ones that when they come cannot be put off!

Sometimes people have the spiritual gift of prayer. But whether prayer is our gift or not, we, like the disciples, each implore Jesus: "Lord, teach us to pray, as John taught his disciples" (Luke 11:1). We need to have models for prayer—especially at times when it is difficult for us to form our words to God and focus our attention on God. Yet, Lent is a time given to us for exactly this purpose. We learn to pray in the community as we prepare for the Lord's vindication. Lenten prayer is the crucible for authentic faith.

The prayers offered here as models aim for honesty and integrity before God. Few of these prayers are akin to a "wish list," but are rather sincere words addressed in concert with other worshipers who desire a deeper commitment to one another and to God. Recently I heard an unusual but earnest prayer. The prayer merely was this: "Dear Lord, help me be the kind of person my dog thinks I am. Amen." We have all heard many prayers, and my guess is that this prayer is about as honest as most people could ever muster. Honest prayer makes us open and vulnerable before God and God's mercy.

Accordingly God calls us to be most honest with ourselves and with the divine during the penitential season of Lent. In Lent we also worship ritually with our sisters and brothers in the faith. Many contemporary believers forget to appreciate that when a congregation prays together it shares in a centuries-old ritual. As we offer God our prayers, we reaffirm our bold belief that God hears the prayers of God's people. At times, no doubt, each of us has attended churches where we profoundly sensed the boldness and confidence of the people's prayers. The ritual of prayer is one way we enact our daring faith in God's providence.

In fact, the community of faith often welcomes the role of ritual in its worship life because regular worship is as important to us as the air we breathe. In John Wesley's sermon titled "The Great Privilege of those that are Born of God" he notes what he calls "spiritual respiration." Wesley writes that when a person is born of God, "born of the Spirit the... breath of God is immediately inspired, breathed into the new-born soul... prayer being the breath of every soul which is truly born of God. And by this new kind of spiritual respiration, spiritual life is not only sustained but increased day by day" (*The Works of John Wesley*, vol. 1, sermon 19, edited by Albert C. Outler [Nashville: Abingdon Press, 1984], p. 434). Bold prayers reveal bold believers. Bold believers reveal God's persuasive witness in the world. In all of this the idea is that God breathes into our souls and then our act of breathing sends God's Spirit back out to the world. This is part of what ritual worship and prayer does for us—we breathe God in and out together as the household of faith.

Not only do our worship rituals allow us to breathe in the Spirit of God, but enacting ritual also orients us within our community's social structures. Whether the ritual is a handshake, the singing of an opening hymn, or the reciting of the Apostle's Creed, it helps us participate in community. Worship leaders, armed with the people's prayer concerns, facilitate ritual by offering sacrifices of prayer on the people's behalf. In Jesus we have a high priest who offers sacrifices for us (Hebrews 2:17–3:1). Lent is the time when we reflect most deeply on that atoning sacrifice of Jesus on our behalf. Yet we remember that Jesus did not sacrifice for his own sin, as he was "without sin." Hence, Jesus becomes our eternal high priest. Jesus intercedes for us and prays for us. In Jesus we can approach God's throne with courage because it is Jesus who offers a perfect sacrifice for us. Ritual reminds us about Jesus' place near God's throne of grace. As we pray together in Lent we remind ourselves that like the original disciples "we believers are all in the same boat."

I learned the importance of ritual in my first parish when I altered the order of worship slightly one Sunday morning. It seemed to me that the flow of worship would be better if I switched two of the worship elements. I never thought that anyone would notice because the change I enacted was ever so slight. Yet, after worship, several people commented on how uncomfortable the change had made them. Clearly, change is part of life. But, conversely, this experience helped me recognize that people take the order of worship much more to heart than I had assumed.

Paul, in writing about speaking in tongues, imparted something profound: "All things should be done decently and in order" (1 Corinthians 14:40). Long-standing rituals in social conventions and worship services supply a deep purpose. The purpose of ritual in worship is to invite people to the throne of grace. We now approach this throne with boldness because of Jesus our great High Priest. Worship is the time and the place where we come to the throne of grace.

During Lent our prayers may seem ritualistic. The reason for this circumstance is that during this high holy season of Lent, worship leaders guide people both emotionally and intellectually through difficult times by the use of familiar words and rituals. Leading congregations via familiar prayers and worship elements allows people to negotiate the deep value and meaning that Lent has for us as a season of spiritual preparation.

As you use this diminutive book for devotional purposes, or as you assemble worship materials, bulletins, and guides for people you lead in worship, may the depth of our faith be transparent as we honor God's holy name together. As Jesus walked the Lenten path toward his passion, may we also walk with him during Lent as his faithful followers and devout disciples.

David Neil Mosser
First United Methodist Church
Arlington, Texas 76011
18 June 2010—Saint Fortunatus ("the Philosopher") Feast Day

ASH WEDNESDAY

Invocation (Psalm 51; 2 Corinthians 5–6; Matthew 6)

O Lord, open our hearts that we may acknowledge our failings. Open our lips that we may declare your praise. Although we each fall short, we praise you in the name of Christ who takes away our sin and invites us to walk in the paths of righteousness. May our Lenten fast begin not with dismal faces or with sorrowful frowns, but with faces aglow in the oil of your Holy Spirit. Amen.

Invocation (Joel 2)

God of dust and ash, you fashioned us from the dust of the earth, and to dust we shall return. May the ashes placed upon our foreheads this day remind us of who we are and whose we are. Draw us back to you, O God, for you are gracious and merciful, slow to anger, and abounding in steadfast love. Heal the hardness of our hearts, that we may be faithful disciples of the one who makes all things new. Amen.

Invocation

Loving God, come to us now. Come to those who are lonely and frightened. Come to those who are sick and discouraged. Come to our neighbors and friends. Build us up as your disciples, teaching us truth and showing us how to be a people of love and grace. Amen.

Invocation (Adapted from Psalm 84)

O God, how lovely is your dwelling place. My soul longs for you. Come into this place. Dwell in us. Answer our longing with your presence. Accept our offering of praise. Amen.

Prayer of Confession

Gracious God, we confess that we have not loved you with our whole hearts, and we have not loved our neighbors as we love ourselves. Forgive us, we pray. Open our hearts wide to you, that you might renew our faith and strengthen us for obedient service. Amen.

Prayer of Confession

O God who will not let us go, as we worship this day we confess that we have been so wrapped up in ourselves that we have taken little note of either you or our neighbor who is in need. Forgive us, we pray, when we forget that our own scripture tells us that you, O God, "created humankind in [your] image, in the image of [you, you] created them; male and female [you] created them" (Genesis 1:27). On this Ash Wednesday bring to our consciousness the truth that it is from the dust we came and to the dust we will return. Between these moments of dust, Lord, let us shine as those "crowned...with glory and honor" (Psalm 8:5). Bring this to pass as we pray in Jesus' name. Amen.

Words of Assurance

When we confess our sins, God is faithful and just, cleansing us from all unrighteousness. God is slow to anger and abounding in steadfast love. In the name of Jesus Christ, you are forgiven! In the name of Jesus Christ, you are forgiven!

Prayer of Confession (Psalm 51)

Holy God, wash us thoroughly of our iniquity and cleanse us from our sin; for our transgressions are ever before us and we have done what is evil in your sight. You desire truth in our inward being, yet we turn our backs on the wisdom you would impart in our hearts. Create in us a clean heart, O God, and put a new and right spirit within us. Do not cast us away from your presence, and do not take your Holy Spirit from us. Forgive our sins and lead us in your paths anew that we might teach transgressors your ways and lead sinners to return to you. Amen.

Words of Assurance (Joel 2:12-13)

Hear the words of the prophet Joel: "Yet even now, says the LORD, return to me with all your heart, with fasting, with weeping, and with mourning; rend your hearts and not your clothing. Return to the LORD, your God, for [God] is gracious and merciful, slow to anger, and abounding in steadfast love, and relents from punishing."

Prayer of Confession (Psalm 51)

Merciful God, cleanse us with hyssop; wash us white as snow. You desire truth in our inner being—truth about our many failings: lust (pause), greed (pause), oppression (pause), violence (pause), intolerance (pause), racism (pause). Purge our sins with the atoning hyssop of Christ the Lord. Amen.

Words of Assurance (Joel 2)

The promise of God is clear. When we return to the Lord, God is gracious and merciful, slow to anger and abounding in steadfast love. When we return to the Lord with weeping and fasting, God forgives our sin and blesses us with a renewed and deepened relationship with the Almighty.

Pastoral Prayer

O Lord our God, we praise you above all creatures and all things. We lift prayers of thanks for the amazing fact that you loved us enough to give yourself fully for us. Now we have the challenge of trying to live fully for you. Help us in the task of discipleship. Be our spiritual teacher; remove our thick clouds of ignorance. Help us, O God, to live by the pattern and example given to us by Jesus Christ. Give us an eagerness and joyful desire to obey your command to make disciples of all nations. Send us out with renewed courage to proclaim the faith and hope within us to a world that needs both so that we may become your body in the world. Amen.

Pastoral Prayer

O God in whom we live and move and have our being, as you collect us for worship remind us that we are mortal and you are divine. Too often in our world today, the creature has forgotten the creator. We are at our best, O Lord, when we remember, and we are at our worst when we forget. Give us sacred memory of the order of creation and our place in the order of salvation. May we once again claim our rightful place as stewards of your manifold gifts. In Jesus' name and on this Ash Wednesday, we pray. Amen.

Pastoral Prayer

In the darkness and drear of too much of the high life, Gracious Presence, be for us the light that illumes the truth for our time and place. Frequently we punish ourselves by reaching for things beyond the grasp of what is indeed good for us. As we worship this night bring to mind that we are indeed our sisters' and brothers' keepers. Inspire us to feed others as you have first fed us. As the celebrants apply ashes to our foreheads, make us mindful that you, O God, unite us with all people around the world and through the centuries by our common sin and need of salvation. God, make your deliverance manifest this holy night as you offer us Jesus. Amen.

Offering Prayer (Matthew 6)

Gracious God, we have sought recognition for our piety and taken pride in our giving, congratulating ourselves for caring about our neighbors. Receive these offerings in the spirit of your Son, who taught us that where our heart is, there our treasure will be also. Amen.

Offering Prayer (Psalm 51)

What would make you happy, O God? We know it is not sacrifice. Our cash is cold and hard and heartless as it drops into the offering plate. You have told us what is pleasing: a broken and contrite heart. Receive this day our sacrifice of praise as we give to you from the very depths of our souls. In Jesus' name, we pray. Amen.

Offering Prayer

To you, Author of Benevolence, we owe our gratitude. You have made us all that we are and all we hope to become. Your bounty is too great for us to authentically understand—we can only wonder. Yet, like huffy children, thanksgiving fails to trip easily from our lips. Mostly we function as those who believe that we are the beneficiaries of our own talents and labor. Disabuse us of this notion and make us grateful people once again, in Christ's name. Amen.

Benediction

God guide you this week into the places and unto the people where God needs your voice. In that moment, may you speak the good news, in the name of the Father, and of the Son, and of the Holy Spirit. Amen.

Benediction

And now go into the world, into the uttermost regions, and serve your brothers and sisters. You go with the successes in faith and with the Peters and the Judases as well, in the name of the Father, the Son, and the Holy Spirit. Amen.

Benediction

Expect something new to happen in this Lenten season. Walk through the wilderness with the hope of Christ. Share the gift of friendship and hospitality with others, for this is what our Lord has done for us. Amen.

Benediction (Psalm 51)

Wash us thoroughly from our iniquities and we will be whiter than snow. Bathe us in your steadfast love. Create in us a clean heart, O God, and help us hear the joy of your calling. Restore to us the joy of your salvation. Go with God's blessing. Amen.

First Sunday in Lent

Invocation (Luke 4)

God, our Guide and Guardian, lead us on this journey of faith. Through the days and weeks of Lent, help us walk your path to the cross; strengthen us to resist the demons that would lead us astray. Walk with us, Christ Jesus. Be our shelter and our salvation, even as we seek to be your disciples.

Invocation (Genesis 9; Psalm 25)

Loving God, we lift up our souls and search for your promised presence. Reveal yourself to us this day—in mighty mountains, in brilliant rainbows, in curious creatures, in spring rain showers, in joyous children, in grieving friends, in challenging scriptures, in meaningful prayers, in repentances and forgiveness, in love and grace. Teach us your ways. Lead us in your truth. Guide us on the Lenten journey toward the darkness of death and the hope of resurrection. In the name of the risen Christ, we pray. Amen.

Invocation

We come before you, O God, seeking strength and courage for our lives and the life of this fellowship. We pray for such spiritual reinforcement as would guide us safely through the times of temptation in life. Grant us such powers of discernment that we may not yield to temptations that look good but will erode our souls. Amen.

Prayer of Confession

Our gracious God, Jesus taught us to love you with all our heart, soul, mind, and strength. Jesus taught us to love our neighbors as ourselves. Jesus taught us to trust you completely. We confess that we have often failed to learn, and what we have learned we have often failed to put into practice. Forgive us, we pray, in the name of Jesus, the great teacher. Amen.

Words of Assurance

Hear the good news: God is ever more ready to forgive than we are to acknowledge our need for forgiveness. Receive God's gift of forgiveness in Christ and walk in newness of life.

Prayer of Confession

We confess, O God, that we are attracted to false gods and easy answers in life. We are vulnerable to temptations that could damage us in ways that are not obvious. Forgive us that sin draws us like moths to a flame. Restore us and fill us with godly resolve. In Jesus' name, we pray. Amen.

Words of Assurance

Hear the good news: Christ died for our sins and rose again that God may free us from the tyranny of judging others to live fully in the power of God's grace. In the name of Jesus Christ, God forgives your sins and offers you a transformed future. Live fully into God's grace. Amen.

Prayer of Confession

Gracious God, we confess that we often lose sight of the hope we have in you. Our failures and our self-doubts preoccupy our thoughts and paralyze us from your work. We feel at times intimidated and useless in making a difference in the world. We pray for your forgiveness and we ask for your help so that we might be steadfast and faithful to you. Help us focus on what you have given us in Jesus, in whose name we pray. Amen.

Words of Assurance

God sees, even when we have lost sight. God is steadfast and faithful. God forgives. Thanks be to God. Amen.

Prayer of Confession (Luke 4)

Gracious God, you know the difficult paths we tread; you know the challenges we face. Forgive us when we wander away from your guidance. Reclaim us when we seek other gods that lead to our own destruction. Guide us back to you that we may rest in your shelter. Strengthen our resolve that we may face the demons of our lives and courageously resist the temptations that blind us to your love. In hope and trust, we pray. Amen.

Words of Assurance (Romans 10)

Because we trust in the midst of our doubt, God lays a path before us. Because we hope in the face of our sin, salvation is ours! In the name of Christ, God forgives all and reclaims us as God's holy children.

Pastoral Prayer

Creator God, we thank you for the gift of life itself. We know that everything you created is good and that our lives can be purposeful and meaningful. We confess that we often fall short of the mark. We turn against your ways and by doing so we cause your good and orderly creation to sink back into the chaos from which you created it. We know that you are a forgiving God, slow to anger and abounding in steadfast love. Forgive us and restore us unto you. Help us enjoy the goodness of your creation and allow your light and love to shine through us; for it is in your Son's name, Jesus Christ, we pray. Amen.

Pastoral Prayer

Gentle Jesus and loving Lord God, here we are again today, hoping that the sanctity of this place will reinforce the sincerity of our petitions. Here we are again today, sitting in the same place, asking the same questions, and even confessing the same sins. Unworthy though we may be in our own sight, and perhaps in the sight of others, we remember that you regard us as persons of worth no matter how much nonsense we have dragged our lives through to get here. So, here we are, Lord—again. We know that in this brief time we cannot find answers to all the questions our minds can frame, or heal all the hurts our hearts have sustained, or untie all the knots in our lives; but we pray that you will help us get started. In Jesus' name, we pray. Amen.

Pastoral Prayer

We acknowledge, O God, our difficulty in being honest with you and ourselves, much less with other people. We admit how often we try to look better than we really are. It seems to be a part of our dark side to pose and feign and give artificial impressions. And we do not do it entirely in the interest of peacekeeping and diplomacy. Excuse us that so much of our insincerity has to do with pretense, face-saving, and masking the true feelings we are afraid to express and face. Help us, O God, come to terms with the dark dimensions of our natures so destructive to others and ourselves. Uncertain of our worth, our God-given dignity, and ourselves, we are afraid of honest anger and constructive criticism that seek to right wrongs. As we give voice to our personal and community affirmations, hear our deep desire to control our anxious feelings rather than let them control us. Enter into the ambivalence that tears us apart and damages so many important relationships. Help us to such honesty in attitude and selfhood that we will be able to reconnect all the fragmented parts of life; but most of all remind us that as whole people we can share the whole gospel with a hurting world. In Jesus' name, we pray. Amen.

Pastoral Prayer (Psalm 25)

God of hope and help, show us your ways. Lead us in your truth. Do not remember the sins of our youth, or the sins of this past week. Even as we remember the error of our ways, we ask for your forgiveness and your grace. Help us know you so completely that we may walk in your paths of love and righteousness, and live in the light of your grace. Make us once again the people you first created us to be, O God, and put your hand on our shoulder to guide us in right paths. Make us mindful of the needs of others and give us the courage to represent the right as well as the righteous ones in our midst. Grant us during this Lenten season a truer perspective not only of who you are, but also who we are as created in your image. In Jesus' name, we pray. Amen.

Offering Prayer (Luke 4)

Gracious God, we bring this offering for a world that needs more than bread. Transform our dollars and coins into your gifts: bread for the journey, food for the hungry, hope for the despairing, and opportunity for the discouraged. Transform our lives that we may walk with Christ and offer your love to the world. Amen.

Offering Prayer (Genesis 9)

In gratitude and praise, we remember the many gifts of your creation and of your covenant with us. Accept these gifts we bring, that others may find in them signs of your love and grace. Gather these gifts and the gifts of our lives. Color them with hope and joy, that in our giving and in our living a brilliant rainbow of love may shine forth. In Christ's name, we pray. Amen.

Offering Prayer

As you, O God, who have given us much, stand as our benefactor, may we, who have received much, show compassion and a sense of urgency as we share with those who are your children too. Bless not only those who receive, Lord, but also bless those who give. Amen.

Benediction

May the God who walks beside us in our wilderness wanderings walk beside us this day as we leave this place to be the children of God in a world crying out for meaningful rituals and reminders of hope in the midst of chaos and distress. Take God's hope as you depart in Jesus' name. Amen.

Benediction

Now may the God of the journey, the One who creates us, redeems us, and sustains us, keep you this day and forever. May you continue to celebrate the bounty that God provides, and may you be faithful to continue following wherever the path may lead. Amen.

Benediction

Go forth with the strength and courage witnessed in the lives of Peter and John. Be faithful on your journey of discipleship. Live with the kind of hope and love that empowers and encourages others, just as you have been empowered and encouraged by the Spirit of God. Amen.

Benediction

God sends you into the world like Jesus told those disciples before us: "Go on your way. See, I am sending you out like lambs into the midst of wolves" (Luke 10:3). Yet we go into the world knowing that Jesus is the sheepfold and the shepherd who protects us all. Amen.

Second Sunday in Lent

Invocation

You have brought us from many places to this place of worship, O God. We have come from home and work, from disappointment and success, from our past and into our future. By your Spirit stir our imaginations to worship you as the Holy One in our midst whose great dream for our lives is to become your sons and daughters through Jesus Christ our Lord. Amen.

Invocation

Lord Jesus Christ make us mindful of your presence. When we grope in darkness, show us your light. With all the stain of the week past and all the hurt we carry to worship, we need for you to make us new again. We do not ask you to be present for we know you are. Instead we ask that you will enable us to be aware of your presence and be born anew in your grace. Amen.

Invocation

God, you are our God of hope, faith, and love. We find renewal in you so that we might soar as eagles and do your work on this earth. As we gather this morning for worship, fill us with your Spirit of encouragement and teach us to be your people by sharing your good gifts to the world. Amen.

Invocation (Genesis 17)

God of promise, we come as your people, rejoicing in the abundance of your love. Give us faith to answer your call. Strengthen us to hope against hope. Guide us into a deep and abiding trust. Lead us on a journey toward wholeness that we may become your holy people, faithfully doing your will. Amen.

Prayer of Confession (Mark 8)

Gracious God, we want to hold on to what we know. We are afraid to take risks for the sake of the gospel; we want to keep our lives safe. Forgive us, O God, when we cling to comfort, when we build barriers to protect ourselves, when we choose the easy way. Transform our fears that we may deny ourselves, take up our cross, and follow Jesus to serve the world. Amen.

Words of Assurance (Mark 8; Romans 4)

Those who risk their lives for the sake of Jesus Christ will inherit the world.

Prayer of Confession

Forgiving God, we confess how we have rebelled against you. We have allowed doubts and fears to hold us back from the freedom to which you have called us in Christ Jesus our Lord. We have been quick to blame others for our weakness and slow to accept responsibility for ourselves. Forgive us, and grant us your peace, through Jesus Christ our Lord. Amen.

Prayer of Confession (Genesis 15; Psalm 27)

Eternal God, we are swift to join Abram's doubt and impatience but we find it difficult to copy Abraham's faith and trust. We want to believe your promises but the here-and-now problems of daily life consume our focus and erode our faith. Open our eyes to your light. Open our hearts to your love. Open our minds to your possibilities. Speak to us today, O God, and strengthen our faith, that we, too, may know the everlasting power of your love. We pray this in the name of Jesus. Amen.

Words of Assurance (Psalm 27)

When God is with us, whom shall we fear? The God of salvation will never forsake you. God's patience knows no limits. Wait for the Lord. Be strong and take heart.

Prayer of Confession

Almighty God, we confess that we are incurable scorekeepers. We judge others with a standard we never use for ourselves. We see the speck in others' eyes while ignoring the ugly log in our own. "Forgive us," we pray. Forgive us for ever thinking we could be, even for one moment, the measure of righteousness or the standard of justice. As the cross of Christ casts its long shadow over our Lenten journey, call us again to lives of genuine penance and amendment of life. By your grace and through your transforming love, make us the people you have fashioned us to be, your sons and daughters, through Jesus Christ our Lord. Amen.

Pastoral Prayer

On this Sabbath day, as we journey with Jesus toward the Lenten cross, O God, we pray not only for ourselves but for others—many others, known and unknown, named and unnamed—from whose lives health or happiness has fled, leaving hollow remnants of the persons they once were. Make us more eager to help others than to criticize or give them bits of our wisdom that we think they need. Help us learn by heart what Jesus knew so well: the hungry, the hurt, the sick, and the oppressed do not care about how much we know until they know about how much we care. Touch our lives with grace through the worship we experience here today. In the good name of Jesus we pray to you who makes the light shine out of darkness. Amen.

Pastoral Prayer

Almighty God, Father of our Lord Jesus Christ, we come before you today, in the silhouette of the cross, to offer the prayers of this congregation. We thank you for the hope we have that is born of our faith in Jesus. How grateful we are for the sacrifice Jesus made for us, and for the example for living we see in Jesus' life. Grant us the strength and courage to follow him closely. We confess how we have failed you by our commitment to lesser values and selfish goals. Open our eyes to what is of lasting value in this world and the next. In Christ's name, we pray. Amen.

Pastoral Prayer

Lord, you call us to follow you wherever you lead. We want to listen to your guidance but we are so comfortable in our present situation. You know, nevertheless, that sometimes being comfortable isn't comforting. So take us to new places of faith and action. Guide and direct our paths for your sake. May this journey of faith take us to people and places that need your care, and may our journey be more fulfilling than we could have ever imagined. It is in Jesus' name that we pray. Amen.

Offering Prayer (Genesis 15; Luke 13)

Faithful God, you have kept your promises to us. Our lives give witness to your abundant blessings. May we faithfully keep our promises to you. Strengthen our commitment to live as true disciples of Jesus Christ. Your love sustains us, guides us, and empowers us.

Take these gifts as signs of our promise to give ourselves completely into your care—to live without fear, to trust your love without reservation. Amen.

Offering Prayer (Genesis 17; Romans 4; Mark 8)

God of the ages, from generation to generation you have blessed us with life and abundant love. We have a rich inheritance of faith. Use the gifts we bring to restore hope to the hopeless and faith to those who despair. We would give what we have that we may follow you with all our heart. Amen.

Offering Prayer

Our Father of Lights, remind us that Paul used himself as an example to those in the Book of Acts—especially as he urged the support for the weak. May we heed the apostle's words as he quotes Jesus: "It is more blessed to give than to receive" (Acts 20:35). Amen.

Benediction

May Christ always lift the darkness of your life, and the Spirit blow afresh through your hearts, and may God's light dispel your darkness this day and evermore. Amen.

Benediction

As you go, remember that you are now people of the journey. You are not finished products; rather, God is transforming your lives each day. As you follow Jesus, remember to pick up your cross daily, for it is only through the cross that we find everlasting life. Go, and take your new name, "Christian," for the journey! Amen.

Benediction

And now may the God who created all that is birth such a new dream in our lives that we will joyfully serve others in the power of grace. And may the blessing of God—the Father, the Son, and the Holy Spirit—rest upon us all now and until we meet again. Amen.

Benediction (Genesis 17; Romans 4)

Grow strong in faith as you glorify God. Live in the assurance of God's promises. May the abundance of God's blessings be with you now and forever.

THIRD SUNDAY IN LENT

Invocation

God, we know you are already with us in this time of worship, welcoming us not as travelers who visit once in a while, but as your cherished children. Help us center our hearts so that we may hear your voice as we give back our time and energy to you. Amen.

Invocation

Living Christ, we often go to the well. We too often find ourselves parched by the pressures of life and in need of refreshment for body and soul. May we, like the Samaritan woman, discover you during the dry moments of our lives. Come to us and draw for us the living water of your presence. We pray in your holy name. Amen.

Invocation (Psalm 63; 1 Corinthians 10)

Lord of overflowing abundance, you are our God. Our souls thirst for you like travelers in a dry and weary land. We praise you with joyful lips and bless you with uplifted hands. Guard us when we stand for what is right, lest we fall to our disgrace. Test our courage in the face of evil, and save us from the time of trial, that we may be worthy disciples of your Son, our rock and our foundation. Amen.

Invocation

God, we know you are present in this place long before we begin to prepare our hearts for worship, because you are present in our lives long before we are born. Remain with us as we seek to give back to you a small portion of your generosity to us. Prepare our hearts to worship you, a good and faithful God.

Prayer of Confession

As we move through Lent, O God who is gracious beyond our ability to conceive, help us, as we journey, to recognize those other people who are on their journey too. Save us from insensitivity to the tangible and indefinable hurts of those people who walk past us each day as they too search for truth and meaning. Forgive our sins—even the sin that clings so close and subtle that we scarcely know it is there. Remove our guilt and lead us in lives of daily commitment to the highest and the best we can know. Remind us that the greatest journey we will ever make is the trip from our minds to our hearts. Send your spirit of healing upon us so that we can once again grow into the image in which you created us to be. Give us the healing gift of Jesus that we confess we need so much. We pray this prayer of declaration of sin in the name of Jesus Christ. Amen.

Prayer of Confession

O God of justice, we know that if you examined our lives without divine and loving prejudice then there would be no forgiveness, no mercy, and no absolution from you for our troubled lives. As we gather in this sacred sanctuary, we can only image the stench of our twenty-first-century graven images and idols that cling to us like the overpriced garments we wear. Help us this day confess our sin before you, O God, and before our brothers and sisters who look to us for guidance and leadership. Make us one with you and with one another, for you remind us that we believing folk find our proper unity in our heartfelt confessions of faith. Open us to new experiences, and especially this day send your Holy Spirit upon us to bind us to you and to one another. In the name of the one who gave all for us, we now pray. Amen.

Prayer of Confession (Psalm 19; John 2)

With hearts of sorrow, we come before you, O God, to confess what you already know: we have failed to keep your laws. Again and again we have followed our own selfish will rather than your holy and life-giving will for our lives. We have twisted your decrees and institutions to suit our preconceptions and interests rather than your own. Forgive us, O God, and cleanse us from hidden faults, that the words of our mouths and the meditations of all our hearts may be acceptable to you, our Rock and our Redeemer.

Words of Assurance (Exodus 20)

God shows steadfast love and blesses to the thousandth generation those who walk in God's ways. In love, God sent Jesus to bless and redeem God's people. God forgives us our sins and restores us to new life. Let us rejoice in God's mercy.

Prayer of Confession (Isaiah 55; Psalm 63)

Merciful God, we are so thirsty! Yet when offered refreshment from the waters of life we rely on our own means and end up drinking sand. Heal our hardness of heart and help us seek you while you may be found, that we may abide in your steadfast love now and forevermore. Amen.

Words of Assurance (1 Corinthians 10; Luke 13)

God is our help in times of trial. If we put our trust in Christ, God will help us stand. Even if we have not borne good fruit in the past, Christ works to help us bear good fruit in the time before us.

Pastoral Prayer

Almighty God, our heavenly Father, whose way is mercy and whose name is love, we come today in grateful praise for the blessings that have fallen upon our lives from your hand. You have blessed us a thousand times when we didn't deserve it—and sometimes when we didn't notice it. Keep us ever mindful of the source of all the good things that have come to us. We lift the needs of your people today in prayer. We pray not only for those of us here in this sanctuary. We pray for all who are apart from us, wherever they are. We pray for those who are estranged, lost, and missing from our fellowship. We pray for those who once found meaning in worship but who now wander restlessly in the contemplation of temporal things. We pray for those who have never known what it means to believe that God cares and who have never experienced a relationship that made them feel anyone cares. May the loving intent of this church reach the hearts and lives of the lonely, the lost, and the estranged. We pray for the sick and the hurt today, whoever they are and wherever they may be. We pray for those who suffer undiluted physical, spiritual, or emotional pain daily. This we pray in the strong name of the Master, Jesus Christ, our Lord. Amen.

Pastoral Prayer

O God, hear us as we pray. Walk the corridors of our hearts. Grant us the courage to take time to be holy, even now as we wait for you and listen for you. Too many of us have been drawn close to you for years but have never taken that last step of taking off our sandals to be vulnerable before you, to say from the depths of our souls, "O God, I need you." Those of us who handle the holy so frequently, who traffic in God language and church culture, who carry scriptures in our hands, and who walk among one another as brothers and sisters long for this experience of holiness in our lives. Grant us the courage to strip off all that is protective so that we may allow your spirit to do its work within our souls. In the name of Jesus, we pray. Amen.

Pastoral Prayer

Almighty God, Father and Mother of us all, we seek your favor and guidance as we try to strengthen our spiritual lives. We know that you, O God, made us in your image, but some days we feel that you need to remake us. Somewhere along the way we have lost or obscured some essential elements of your divinity, and we sorely miss what we have lost. You made us in love, but we let bitterness take root in us and we let hate grow. You made us merciful and kind, but we have permitted jealousy to ruin that spirit. You made us people of reason, but our passions rule us. You made us just and loving toward others, but we devise ways to get even with and ahead of our brothers and sisters. Remake us, O Lord, in your image. In the name of the Messiah, we pray. Amen.

Offering Prayer

As we gather this day, O Lord of all, if we are honest we recognize that we are beneficiaries of all that we have had, will have, and have now in this sacred place and time. As we contemplate our degree of gratitude during this Lenten season, give us a generous impulse toward others as we celebrate your gracious benevolence toward us. We pray this in the name of the Suffering Servant, Jesus Christ. Amen.

Offering Prayer (1 Corinthians 1)

The wisdom of the world tells us to hoard what we own, O God, while you invite us to share what we have with those in need. Accept these gifts for your purposes, that we may be your servants in the world.

Offering Prayer (Luke 13)

Loving God, you have set the table and have given us every good thing. In gratitude for your kindness and mercy, receive our thanks and offerings. Accept our hearts into your keeping, that our lives may bear good fruit as we pray to enter into your glory. Amen.

Benediction

Go in peace, for you do not go alone. God goes with you. Go in peace, for when your path leads into the wilderness remember that Jesus Christ has been there before you. Go in peace to bless others along the way and to receive their blessing. Amen.

Benediction

And now may the one who has welcomed you here and met you in transforming love send you from this place of worship to the place of service, and may you be made new by the power of

Jesus Christ our Lord, who lives and reigns with God and the Holy Spirit, one God, forever and ever. Amen.

Benediction

Go into the world and be unpredictable. Be the one who sees a need and responds. Hear the words of Jesus and go and do likewise.

Benediction

Having drunk deeply of the living water of Jesus Christ our Lord, go now into Christ's world to give water to the thirsty there.

Fourth Sunday in Lent

Invocation

Holy Lord, led by God's Spirit into the wilderness, guide us to where you would have us go. Teach us the value of the Way and let us follow the path that you have laid before us. Amen.

Invocation

O Lord, we journey these roads of Lent and more and more see ourselves in the people Jesus encountered on the roads of his life. We do not always like what we see. Jesus keeps calling for us to repent. He offers to clean the mud from our eyes that we might see him clearly. When we see Jesus clearly, the divine changes us. When we see our world clearly, God calls us to change it. O Lord, help us see. Fashion us as the people you desire us to be. In Jesus' name, Amen.

Invocation

Great Triune God, we have gathered here in your name as an act of faith, believing that you are not only among us but that you also love us. It is often hard to recognize your love, see your mercy, and feel your presence. Help us today in our worship that we might be transparent to your grace as you reveal yourself to each one of us. Amen.

Invocation (Joshua 5; 2 Corinthians 5; Luke 15)

God of forgiveness and grace, thank you for your warm and loving welcome. Open our hearts that we may receive your grace and peace. Bless us and renew us that we may live as new creations. Inspire us to be your kingdom on this earth that we may be your promised land—with actions that nourish like milk, with words that soothe like honey. Amen.

Prayer of Confession (Luke 15)

God of grace and love, forgive us when we wander away from your promises; forgive us when we withhold from others the forgiveness we seek for ourselves. Welcome us into your loving embrace. Warm us with your grace that we may reach out with loving arms to a world in need of your compassion, a world in need of your love. In Christ's name, we pray. Amen.

Words of Assurance (1 Corinthians 5; Luke 15)

Rejoice! She who was lost has been found. Sing aloud! He who was dead is alive. In Christ, you are a new creation. In Christ, you are a new creation.

Prayer of Confession (Numbers 21)

God, we have sinned against you. We have spoken against you and your servant Jesus. We have uttered lies. We have cursed you and others. We have said vulgar things. We have let doubt consume us. We have let the serpent's venom and hatred in our world bite us. We have oppressed the helpless. We have been intolerant of others. We have delighted in violence. We have spent money foolishly. Please, Lord God, forgive us our transgressions that you may heal us of our sin.

Words of Assurance (John 3)

Hear now the loving truth of God: God did not send the Son into the world to condemn the world, but that God might save the world through him. Those who believe in him are not condemned.

Prayer of Confession

Gracious God, doubt can be so troubling to us. Forgive us when we have failed to understand another's doubt and have not given that person a safe place to share it. Forgive us when we have failed to allow another person to work through his or her doubt and so grow stronger. Forgive us, God, when we have made doubt a destination and have become complacent in seeking your presence, your will, and your way for our lives. Lord, we believe. Help our unbelief. In the name of Jesus we ask this. Amen.

Words of Assurance

Hear the good news. Our mighty God is far more willing and able to forgive than we are to ask. When we turn to God, God hears our prayers and forgives us. This is God's amazing gift of grace.

Prayer of Confession

We confess, O God, that we have filled our lives with poor beginnings and bad endings. We have intended to do and be better than we are. We have wished for good outcomes, but we have not followed the disciplines that would make them so. Forgive our negligence of those ways we know from the life and teachings of Jesus Christ our Lord, in whose name we pray. Amen.

Pastoral Prayer

Dear God, we come here today to praise you and ask you to help us, at least for the time it takes us to pray, set our minds on your blessings and give up feeling sorry for ourselves. You have blessed us with the gift of life—surrounded us with friends, trusted us with responsibility, provided for our needs, and set your love over us. In the quiet of this moment, Lord, we pause to remember those whose sacrifices have secured the goods that we enjoy—parents, teachers, soldiers, inventors, scholars, pioneers, and prophets. But mostly we remember Jesus Christ—his selfless life, his voluntary death, his victorious resurrection, and his continuing power to save. We pray this morning for those who live with a sense of running out of what they need:

- those who are running out of time with their dreams still unfulfilled;
- those who are running out of patience, wondering how long they can endure;
- those who are running out of health, who feel their powers waning;
- those who are running out of money, fighting rising costs on a fixed income;
- those who are running out of excuses, nearing the time when they must assume blame for their failures;
- those who are running out of love, finding it easier to accuse and criticize and hate.

O Lord, you alone can keep us from fading. Fill us again, we ask, for we want to endure to the end. Lead us in paths of love and service. In the name of Jesus, we pray. Amen.

Pastoral Prayer

Gracious, loving God, you know our hearts better than we know them ourselves. You know our certainties and our doubts. Help us see through the pain and uncertainty of doubt to renewed and strengthened faith on the other side of doubt. Enable the doubt within us to stir us up and spur us on to deeper faith, through Christ our Lord. Amen.

Pastoral Prayer

O God, we pray to you as the divinely benevolent mystery, and yet we have reputable glimpses of your grandeur in scripture and most completely in your Son Jesus our Christ. In our finitude we struggle not only with your identity but also with our own. Yet despite our lack of comprehension about so many things divine and human, we pray that you might offer to us the assurance of your heavenly care and compassion toward us, your creatures who live in the guise of children. As we search high and low for our identity we pray we might recognize that too often in our search we neglect our baptismal names. Help us grow into them with grace and mercy. Give us the wherewithal to claim our name and identity as those baptized in the name of the Father, Son, and Holy Spirit. Make us those who wear the moniker of "Christian" as we might wear a pair of well-worn shoes. Guide us as we travel on the path that leads to you. In Christ's name, we pray. Amen.

Invitation to the Offering (Luke 15)

We, whom God invites to throw a feast for the prodigals of our world, have ourselves feasted on God's gift of gracious love. Come! Bring your greatest gifts, your richest jewels, and your most scrumptious food! Offer God your very best, for God has given us the very best in Christ Jesus! Amen.

Offering Prayer (Luke 15)

Mother and Father God, we are poor and lowly, rich and blessed, gifted and graced, downtrodden and unsure. We come as we are, offering you all that we have and all that we are. In Christ Jesus we are reconciled to you, made new by your grace, and gifted by your love. Use these gifts we bring before you as signs of your love and grace in the world.

Offering Prayer

O God who demands all from us because you have given us all, remind us of the steadfastness of King David, who said, "I will not take for the Lord what is yours, nor offer burnt offerings that cost me nothing" (1 Chronicles 21:24). In our bargain-seeking world today, O Lord, help us understand what sacrifice and giving for the sake of others is all about. We pray this hope in Jesus' name. Amen.

Benediction

Go, carrying your doubts with you until the time comes when you can lay them down and walk with a lighter load. Go with the assurance that God walks with you and helps shoulder all your burdens. We pray in the triune name of the Father, the Son, and the Holy Spirit. Amen.

Benediction

Leave this place knowing how God's story ends. Go with the hope of what is to come. Remember to read the signs. Journey forward in faith and peace with the promise of a faithful and merciful God. Amen.

Benediction

The Creator has invited all of us to the party of a lifetime. Live this life as one who knows the host personally. Invite others to come to the party, for this is a cosmic celebration that no one should miss.

Benediction (Luke 15)

In this new creation God allows the lost to be found. We, who were dead, have been given new life. Go into the world, rejoicing that God has welcomed us home. Go with God's blessing to share that welcome with all!

Fifth Sunday in Lent

Invocation

Awaken from the slumber caused by the world's false truths and empty promises. Enter this place of worship where the grace and truth of God are real and available to all who would accept God's good news as witnessed in the life of our Savior and Friend, Jesus the Christ. Amen.

Invocation

Lord, awaken our hearts to be responsive to you, O God, and how you will work in our lives this day. Help us be alert to the still, small voice you use to whisper in our ears and then give us the strength to go and do the work you would have us do. Amen.

Invocation

Lord, as we move nearer and nearer to the blessed tragedy of the gospel and its truth about you and us, make us ever more discerning. With the dissonance of our world's sound bites and the frequency of them it is difficult for us to ferret out the truth. As

Pilate asks, "What is truth?" may we hold fast to the biblical witness of faith that tells us the good news about Jesus and his love. Amen.

Invocation

As we enter this sacred space at this sacred time, O Lord of creation, show us your holy presence. As we sing, pray, and hear the word read and preached, make us those who have ears to hear and eyes to see. Tune our hearts this day and send us back into the world as those who have genuinely worshiped your sacred name. Amen.

Prayer of Confession

Lord, we confess that we have not always lived up to what you have asked us to do. We have fallen asleep; we have not stayed alert. Forgive us our shortfalls and sleepiness. Help us stay awake to your call in us. Amen.

Prayer of Confession (Isaiah 43; Psalm 126; John 12)

Steadfast God, throughout the ages you have cared for your people. You lead us through the wilderness of despair into a land flowing with joy and hope. You transform our tears into laughter, our sorrow into joy. Yet we fail to trust you. Our fears overwhelm us; our tears drown our hope. Afraid of the future, we cling to memories of the past. Forgive us, O God—when we criticize others, when we are afraid of tomorrow, when we lose hope in your goodness. Give us generous spirits that we may anticipate tomorrow with trust in your goodness and your steadfast love. Amen.

Words of Assurance (Isaiah 43; Psalm 126)

God is doing a new thing: transforming our fears into courage, our tears into joy, and our worries into generosity. We are God's people—a people blessed by divine forgiveness and abundant love.

Prayer of Confession

Gracious God, we confess that we are a people with a short memory. We fail to remember your mighty acts and do not always trust you in times of adversity. Remind us of your powerful love and care, that you might fill us with a valiant and daring faith. Give us these in the name of Jesus, we pray. Amen.

Prayer of Confession

Renew us, Lord; wash us of our wickedness and cleanse us from our sin. Put your law within us and write it on our hearts. Take away our excuses, our protestations of ignorance, and our pathetic insistence that we did not properly understand what we were doing. We long for the day when we will not feel compelled to beg excuses for our deeds. Create in us a clean heart, O God, and put a new and right spirit within us. Do not cast us away from your presence and do not take your Holy Spirit from us.

Pastoral Prayer

Gracious and loving God, there are those who are dwelling in a dry, desolate, and lonely wilderness. As they struggle in the wilderness, help them know that they do not struggle alone. Help them know your presence and find comfort and strength to endure. And help us, O God, remember that you call us to be present in another's wilderness as those called to minister in Jesus' name. Amen.

Pastoral Prayer

O God who gives to faithful children all they need or desire, we come to worship you this day with this expectation in our hearts. Baffled, we watch in awe of your intensity of loyalty to us. Yet we confess that despite your great faithfulness to us, sadly we are not committed—either to you or to the brothers and sisters you offer us for companionship and community. We stumble and fall. We break our word. We recoil from our obligations. We do things that are evil in your sight. We confess that we are fragile, often incapable of the courage to live as your people. We are resistant to your ways and break our covenants with you and with those we love. Help us mend our ways. Help us gaze upon you as an inspiration for fidelity. Help us worship you and be obedient to your commandments and ordinances, for it is in your Son's name that we pray. Amen.

Offertory Prayer

Benevolent God and our divine parent, bring to mind today the wisdom of Proverbs that tells us, "A generous person will be enriched, and one who gives water will get water" (11:25). Thus may our gifts not only bless others, but give you, O God, yet another occasion to bless us as well. Amen.

Offertory Prayer

The community of faith, O Lord of all, is where we gather all our human resources under one roof and under one God. As our congregation pools its resources, give us the good judgment to deploy these gifts effectively and faithfully for our neighborhood and beyond—even to our world. Amen.

Offertory Prayer

Lord, as we rediscover our abundant lives from the Spirit, help us live into "the fruit of the Spirit [which] is love, joy, peace, patience, kindness, generosity, faithfulness, gentleness, and self-control" (Galatians 5:22-23). May we be those who reflect faith by growing a garden of spiritual fruits in the garden of our own lives. Send us the grace to grow in kindness, in Jesus' name.

Benediction

Go in peace, knowing that God comforts us and strengthens us for the wilderness times. And, as God comforts you, go to comfort others in their wilderness times. In the name of the Father, the Son, and the Holy Spirit, Amen.

Benediction

May the Spirit of God bring new life to our old and tired bones. May God knit together and renew our lives this day, equipping us for service and strengthening us for the proclamation of God's amazing acts. May we be prophets of grace in the darkest valleys. Amen.

Benediction

May the mighty God who creates strengthen you throughout this week. May Jesus be your guide and companion in the days ahead. May the Spirit comfort you with deep peace. May the three-in-one unite us all.

Benediction

Now may the God of grace and love lead us toward Jerusalem. May we learn to give sacrificially and abundantly. May the aroma of the perfume inspire each of us to a love more profound, and may we consider the cost and still choose to follow. In Jesus' name, we pray. Amen.

PALM SUNDAY/PASSION SUNDAY

Invocation (Psalm 118; Philippians 2)

God of grace and glory, blessed is your Son, Christ Jesus, and blessed is your holy name. As we bless your name and sing with joy, awaken our ears to hear your word; awaken our hearts to listen for your wisdom. As we rejoice in this day that you have made, help us hear even the hard news of Christ's suffering and death. As we celebrate your presence with palms and praises, guide us to live your teachings, even when the path is both painful and difficult. May your presence flow through us into your world. In the name of your Son, Christ Jesus, we pray. Amen.

Invocation

On this Passion Sunday, O Redeemer, remind us of the length and breadth and distance and time that you will traverse to be our God so that we might become your people. As we worship and sing, send the spirit of hope to us so that we might have assurance of your constant and abiding presence among us. Amen.

Invocation

As a testimony to your faithfulness to us, O King of the universe, you send Jesus on the back of a donkey. Remind us on this glorious day of entry that the same people who shouted at the beginning of Holy Week, "Hosanna in the highest heaven!" are also those who at the end of the week shouted, "Crucify him!" May we be aware as we stand before friends and foes not to betray or deny our Lord as did his closest friends. In Jesus' name, we pray. Amen.

Invocation

As we wave our little branches of palm trees and go out to meet Jesus, O Lord, help us shout, "Hosanna! Blessed is the one who comes in the name of the Lord—the King of Israel!" (John 12:13). Make us mindful that as we reenact the story of the beginning of Holy Week the song in our heart is "Were You There?" In the name of the one who lived and died and rose again, Amen.

Prayer of Confession

We confess, O God, how we love the celebration and personal anonymity of the crowd. We love the smell of victory in the air. Forgive us when we turn and run because the parade did not lead where we thought it might. Forgive us when we leave our principles on the parade ground and follow the crowd instead of following Jesus. Forgive us and restore us in the name of Jesus, our Messiah and Savior. Amen.

Prayer of Confession

We confess that so often we remain silent when we should speak. We watch the injustice all around us. We see the widow's plight. We hear the struggle of the single parent. We watch the effort of the poor. We listen to the news of hatred and destruction. Although our eyes see and our ears hear, we confess that we often do nothing. We say nothing. We feel nothing. But our faith tells us that you call us to be about healing this world and bearing witness to our beliefs. Forgive us when we fail! Help us hear the groaning of your creation. When the stones cry out, may we join in their chorus of praise, for we pray in Jesus' name. Amen.

Words of Assurance

Hear the stones shout! God forgives you! Hear the stones shout out! God forgives you!

Prayer of Confession (Psalm 31; Mark 14–15)

Gracious God, you know our every sorrow, our every need. Hear us as we remember the times when our strength failed us, when our distress led us onto paths of hopelessness and despair. Forgive us when we betray you, when we deny you, when we deride you or mock you. Awaken in us a new resolve to be aware of your call and presence in our lives. Help us stay awake, even when the days are hard and the nights are long. Strengthen us to trust in you and to walk with you, even on this path to the cross. Let your face shine upon us that we may know your steadfast love and trust in your resurrection promises. In Christ's name, we pray. Amen.

Words of Assurance (Psalm 31; Philippians 2)

Know that the Lord is God and that Christ's face shines upon us even when we turn away from God's brightness. Walk in the light, dear friends. Gaze upon the Son and know that in the name of Christ, God forgives us!

Prayer of Confession (Luke 19)

Lord Jesus, we are a fickle people, quick to turn away. We are quick to flock to you when all is well, but we are prone to scatter when there is opposition or criticism. Too often we have kept silent before you, afraid to proclaim your praise. It is easy to join the crowd as you ride triumphantly into Jerusalem—singing our joys and expectations, dancing our hopes and dreams. It is far more difficult to stand by you as the crowd cries for your crucifixion. Forgive our weakness when we turn away. Strengthen us for the journey ahead, as we relive your suffering and death, that we might stay beside you to the end. Give us the courage to shout our hosannas, not only today, but each and every day. Amen.

Pastoral Prayer

God of new beginnings, help us hear the good news that in Christ the old has passed away and the new has come. Help us know that even the darkest wilderness gives way to light and life. We thank you that even when the wilderness is of our own making and we have purposely turned away from you, you await our return as a loving parent awaits the return of a lost child. We pray through Christ our Lord. Amen.

Pastoral Prayer

Today, O God, we gather as people whom you have called and named at our baptism. In days gone by we have been strong and confident, but today our confidence wanes as life becomes more complicated. We feel that our friends often devalue us, and our enemies seem to know the rawest areas in our ego. We feel split into a hundred discrete segments, each competing for our best. We pray for wholeness for ourselves and for all who feel fragmented and broken. We pray healing for all who have been hurt in any of the ways that hurt may happen. Guide us in ministries of healing and help, not only for others but also for ourselves. Help us seek out an atmosphere of love and teach us how to create what we cannot find. In the name of your Son, Jesus Christ, we pray.

Pastoral Prayer

O God, we know that you have watched the passage of thousands of Palm Sunday parades, knowing how short they would be. Forgive us for cheering so loudly when we thought Jesus was going to win one for our side, and for running so quickly when things did not turn out as we thought they would. Deliver us from the worship of false values and selfish goals so that we will not waste our lives on things and thoughts and hopes and dreams that are without eternal significance. Save us from selling the highest and best we know for a few pieces of silver, or for a cheap victory over a perceived enemy or an advantage in some ultimately meaningless competition. Strengthen us for the betrayals and disappointments we will face when we refuse to give in to the temptations that come to all who follow Jesus. We pray for the health of those who are ill in whatever way illness may come in life. In the name of Jesus, we pray as a people of God. Amen.

Invitation to the Offering (Mark 14)

Remembering Mary of Bethany, we come now to pour out our gifts to God. May we remember that the poor are with us still, that our neighbors may need our kindness and generosity even now. May we remember Christ in each face of need, in each cry for help, in each yearning for grace. May we offer our alabaster jars, the gift of our very selves. May we open ourselves and pour out the gifts of the Holy Spirit, living with us, that our gifts may flow with blessing and joy to a world in need.

Offering Prayer

What can we offer that you have not already offered us? What can we do that you have not already done for us? Lord Jesus Christ, in your gifts to us you have provided us the way to live and serve you. In both your triumph and your suffering you deserve our praise. Through the gifts we now offer, we express our longing to serve and to follow wherever you go. Amen.

Offertory Prayer

As Christ dwells in your heart, and mercy is your way of life, be glad in Christ Jesus. And with gratitude at your core, sing psalms of joy, hymns of mirth, and spiritual songs with glee to God in three persons. Amen.

Benediction

Now may the same mind be in you that was in Christ Jesus. Through the gift of the Holy Spirit, may God bless you this day with strength, courage, humility, and compassion. May you be faithful as you seek to follow Jesus. Amen.

Benediction

God has fed us by the word. God has given us the good news of God in Jesus Christ by which we can live. As God fills us with the power of the Holy Spirit, share the table of God's grace with all people just as Jesus did. Thanks be to God. Amen.

Benediction (Mark 15)

Christ is going before us, even now, on the road to the cross. Christ goes before us as the way, the truth, and the life. Let us feel the light of his love, even as we enter the darkness of this Holy Week.

Benediction

Passing from joy into sorrow and on to elation, we come to Christ this holy week. Today is only a part of the story. Jesus' triumph leads to his death, and his death to his resurrection. May the journey of this week lead you into the fullness of Christ's love.

MAUNDY THURSDAY

Invocation (Psalm 116; John 13)

Holy Servant, from the depth of your great love you wash us clean in the waters of life; from the center of your compassion you satisfy our thirst with the cup of salvation. We offer our praise and thanksgiving as we turn to you once again to learn the true meaning of selfless giving and servanthood.

Invocation

Instead of wandering aimlessly, Lord, may we open our eyes to the promised land and open our hearts to accept your guidance. Life can be confusing. You have granted us the gift of choice. May we hear the still, small voice that will lead us in a life of service in your name. Amen.

Invocation

As we gather on this Maundy Thursday, we thank you that you are already here to meet us in our time of need. You have led your people through the centuries and have called them to remember your works. Our memories can fade, but you give us the ability to recall again and again your amazing works. You give us benchmarks to recall so that our faith will be strong, even through the difficult times. Help us make Maundy Thursday a night to remember, a night to value, and a night to praise you for your benevolent deeds toward us. We pray this in the name of the One who gave himself for us this night. Amen.

Invocation

Loving God, as we come into your presence, surround us with your Holy Spirit. Fill us with your nourishing grace that always fulfills. Open our hearts and minds to hear your word and to receive the nourishment you offer.

Prayer of Confession

Merciful God, when we seek to escape the chains of selfishness and indifference that bind us, hasten to our aid. When we turn away from those who suffer persecution and injustice, heal our shut-up hearts. When we turn a blind eye to the hungry and the naked, the sick and the imprisoned, the lost and the brokenhearted, be our vision, O God. We ask this in the name of your Son, who enlivens us with the bread of heaven and the cup of blessing especially on the Maundy Thursday night. Amen.

Words of Assurance (Psalm 116)

The Lord hears our voice and supplications, and offers forgiveness of sins and the fullness of grace. Praise the Lord who is the author of our salvation!

Prayer of Confession (Psalm 116; John 13)

Merciful God, the story of the Passover seems so far removed from our lives, yet our need for salvation is as great as the ancient Hebrews'. Forgive us when we feel entitled to others serving us, while ignoring your call to servanthood. Forgive us when we feel that love is due us, while denying the love we owe others. Move us with your generosity and inspire us with your example. We ask this in the name of your Son who nourishes us with the bread of heaven and enlivens us with the cup of salvation. Amen.

Words of Assurance (John 13)

Just as Jesus washed the feet of the one he knew would betray him, Jesus is here to cleanse us from our sins and bathe us in the waters of salvation.

Prayer of Confession

Our gracious God, Jesus taught us to love you with all our heart, soul, mind, and strength, and our neighbors as ourselves. Jesus taught us to serve as he served us on Maundy Thursday. We confess that we have often failed to learn, and what we have learned we have often failed to put into practice. Forgive us, we pray, in the name of Jesus. Amen.

Prayer of Confession

We confess, O Lord, that like the disciples of old we have let pride of place and lust for power slip in the back door of our lives and spoil our devotion to Jesus who was a servant-savior. Worse still, we have hidden these vices in euphemistic cloaks to make them appear good and have welcomed them in the front door of our lives. Save us, O Lord, from these and all other sins of self that evade our commitment to the one who could have had it all but who chose to be a servant instead—Jesus Christ, in whose name we pray. Amen.

Prayer of Confession

O God, this night of Holy Thursday is so much like our real lives. First we ascend to the higher heights as we eat a final meal with Jesus and things seem so—dare we say it—hopeful. Then as the evening wears on we recognize that one of the inner circle will betray Jesus and the whole passion ending begins to unfold. God of grace and great glory, we pray that you continue to sustain us as your expectant people who praise your holy name. We gather this night to celebrate your grace and to hear your word, as disappointing as this night may turn out. Open our eyes to see what you would have us see; open our minds to learn what only you can teach us; open our wills to joyfully serve you and others, through Jesus Christ our Lord—who lived and died that we might have life. Amen.

Pastoral Prayer

God of humility and grace, walk with us through this Holy Week journey. Gather us at your table, and fill us with your grace. Help us live as people who serve and love. Guide us to be disciples who stay awake, even through dark and troubling times. Strengthen us to be disciples who are steadfast and true. In Jesus' name, we pray. Amen.

Pastoral Prayer

God of grace and God of glory, how we thank you on this Maundy Thursday, for you are yet among us as One who serves. We confess that all too often we have been entangled by the snares of our consumer society, caught up in the web of looking for what the world can do for us rather than what we can do for others. We have allowed ourselves to become people who demand much but give little, who expect everything yet give back nothing—even when it comes to our faith in you. So forgive us, we pray, and by your mercy show us the joy of true servant-hood. Allow us to see others from the feet down as we learn to care for them according to your example. When you stand before us one day, offering to wash our feet, may we throttle our misplaced pride long enough lest we have no part with you, O Lord; for all this we pray in your blessed name. Amen.

Pastoral Prayer

As Jesus had his Seder meal with the disciples, remind us that tonight is part of that great story that allows us to pass over from death to life. As the Hebrew children remembered their meal of unleavened bread, may the bread of affliction we eat tonight help us also to "do this in remembrance" of Jesus, reflecting God's great love for us. And even as the Hebrews departed from the land of Egypt, may we too depart from a land of vacuous and meaningless existence. Teach us once again that we are one another's greatest gifts and that sometimes all our toys do is simply keep us distracted and divided from other people. As Jesus urged the disciples to "love one another," may we also heed that divine word tonight as we remember Maundy Thursday in Jesus' name.

Invitation to Foot Washing (John 13)

Loving Christ, on that night long ago you knew that your hour had come; you knew what lay ahead of you. Although your disciples loved and followed you, they would all fail you—one would deny you and one would betray you. Yet you got on your knees, and without judgment or resentment you washed their feet as a servant—even the feet of your betrayer. We have also loved and followed you, and we have also failed you. We cannot comprehend the love that heals us, the love that completes us, the love that sets us free. Through this ritual of a foot-washing ceremony, may we dedicate ourselves to follow your example and be servants of all people. Amen.

Offering Prayer (Luke 4)

Loving Servant, you feed our spiritual hunger with the bread of life; you satisfy our holy thirst with the cup of salvation. We return thanks for washing our feet and for bringing us into full fellowship with you and all God's people. We offer you our very selves, that we may fulfill your law of love. Amen.

Offertory Prayer

As we bring our first fruits and offerings to your throne of grace, O God of the ages, accept them as a sign of our part of the human-divine covenant that you have made with those who call on your holy name. Bless not only we who give these gifts but also those who receive this small portion of our great bounty. We pray this in the name of the one who offered his life for us that we may live in abundance. Amen.

Benediction (Psalm 116; John 13)

Christ's love has washed us clean. Christ has chosen us as his own. Christ's love has fed us with the bread of life and nourished us with the cup of salvation on this Maundy Thursday night. Christ has brought us the gift of God's heavenly banquet. Christ's love has brought us the gift of God's kingdom. Christ has sealed us in his love.

Benediction

Jesus washes clean and bathes our feet with the waters of eternal life. Christ has washed us clean. The One who feeds our spirits is also the One who blesses us with the bread of heaven. Christ has blessed us. The One who revives our souls with the cup of salvation is also the One who loves us. Christ has sealed us in his love.

Benediction

As we go, let us remember God's good works in our lives. Let us give thanks for the leadership that God freely offers. May we walk in trust and faith, knowing that the God who passed over the Israelites will always take care of those who follow God. Now may the God who gives us memories of Maundy Thursday call us back to this place again to worship and praise. Amen.

Benediction

Go and take up the basin of Christ, serving God and your neighbor in all that you do. And may the peace of Christ the servant be with you now and forevermore. Amen.

GOOD FRIDAY

Invocation

Almighty God, as we meet on this day called Good Friday, help us feel our way into the story of Jesus' suffering and passion. Help us recognize Jesus' sacrifice upon the cross and help us live more faithfully in the cross' shadow. As we look upon the distress and misery of our brothers and sisters, make us mindful of the great gift of sacrifice that Jesus performed on our behalf.

Invocation

God of light, into the darkness of this day make us people who are willing to pour out ourselves for others in the spirit by which Jesus poured out himself for us. In this time of worship, O God, help us connect ourselves to the saints of the church, those sisters and brothers who lived full and faithful lives. We pray this in the name of Jesus, who gave us all so that we could have all in his holy name. Amen.

Invocation

O God, into your mystery we dare to enter on this evening of suffering, denial, and death. Give us ears to hear once again the power and beauty of a love that surrendered everything and sacrificed all on this day we call Good Friday. Stir in us such love as we seek to live in your Spirit. Claimed by your courage and strength, move us beyond our fear. Help us as we dare to follow you wherever you may lead us this evening. In the name of Jesus our Lord, we pray. Amen.

Invocation (Psalm 22)

Merciful God, we cry out to you, for you are holy. Come quickly to hear our prayer. Stand in the midst of our congregation, that we may know your presence. Show us your promised salvation, even on this day when hope seems to die and despair seems to rule.

Prayer of Confession (Psalm 22; Hebrews 10)

We have pierced the sides of our brothers and sisters, O God, with the arrows of bigotry, hatred, neglect, and gossip. Our bones are out of joint with sin; we stumble around, unable to walk in love with you and with our neighbors. Heal us, we pray. Forgive our sins that we pour out to you like water. Wash us clean through the sacrifice of our Lord, Jesus Christ, that we may be a redeemed people, marked by your love and mercy. In Jesus' name, we pray. Amen.

Assurance of Pardon (Hebrews 10)

It is through Christ's death that the cross takes on your sins. Because of his death, Jesus forgives all of us of our sins. As a forgiven people your sins and misdeeds God remembers no more. In the name of Jesus Christ, God forgives you your sins!

Prayer of Confession (Isaiah 53)

We, like sheep, have gone astray: we have turned to our own way, we have denied your presence, we have betrayed your truth, and we have laid our iniquities upon you. Forgive us and guide us back into your holy presence. As forgiven followers may we be made new in your grace. As sheep of your pastures may our lives exalt you for the entire world to see! In faith and trust, we pray. Amen.

Words of Assurance (Isaiah 53)

Surely Christ has borne our infirmities and carried our diseases. By his bruises, God heals us. By his love, God makes us whole.

Prayer of Confession

Good Lord, Father and Mother of us all, hear our confession of sin as we look back in time and try to get some fix on why we are like we are. As we mingle with the cast of that doleful drama of

Good Friday, we confess that we find ourselves to be so much like many of them. We confess to being detached bystanders. We confess to being like Judas the betrayer and like the disciples on the run. So much of us is strewn up and down the via dolorosa—and at the front of the cross too. Can we ever get over it all and make a fresh start? Help us, Lord! Amen.

Prayer of Confession

Christ of compassion and kindness, we confess that often we avoid this Friday because we want to feel good. On this Good Friday, forgive us for seeking after feelings that flee and things that don't satisfy. Help us embrace the goodness of this day. Help us embrace the peace and joy that your compassion and love offer to us. In your gracious name, we pray. Amen.

Words of Assurance

Know that our good God has given every good thing to us—forgiveness and love being the greatest gifts of all. Know without a doubt that these good gifts are ours to claim through Jesus Christ. Amen.

Pastoral Prayer

In the darkness of the day and in the darkness of our sanctuary, O God of mercy and charity, help us quiet the inner cauldron of emotions we feel when we ponder Jesus' cross. Help us receive the gift of your unspeakable grace as we distinguish the unconditional love from the many other kinds of provisional loves we embrace. It is, of course, this unconditional love that Jesus not only offers us but also demonstrates for us plainly on this Good Friday. As we ponder the stations of the cross, put us in the place of the disciples who all fled in panic and grief. When Jesus speaks of betrayal, we, like the disciples, ask, "Is it I, Lord?" Help us this day, O God, to own up to our failure of nerve and accept our part in the passion story. Help us learn from the mistakes and experiences of those who have gone before us. Help us remember and appropriate the words of the psalmist who prayed to you: "Create in me a clean heart, O God, and put a new and right spirit within me" (Psalm 51:10). Grant us peace at this time when there seems to be so little peace. In Christ's name, we pray. Amen.

Pastoral Prayer

On this night of pain and sorrow, O God, come and speak to the misery of our hearts. Give us the assurance of faith that despite all evidence to the contrary you alone are King of the universe. Too often like Jesus we cry out in our pain, "My God, my God, why have you forsaken me?" Yet, those who trust your providence know that you have always been our help in times past. Therefore, in the confidence of faith, may we grasp the eternal promises you have given us in Jesus Christ. As we anticipate future joy, may we measure that joy against the ache and angst we now feel. Dear Lord, we know how the Jesus story ends, yet in this moment we are none too sure. Help our doubt and moments of unbelief. Help us cling to Jesus' words that our task as disciples is to love one another as Jesus has loved us. Offer to us those wonderful words of life as we sit in the midst of death, betrayal, and denial. Give us the hope to which your whole creation points. We pray this prayer in Jesus' holy name. Amen.

Pastoral Prayer

Lord of all, we've come today because we cannot escape the truth any longer. We've come because we know that it is our sins that led you to the cross and your love for each of us that kept you there. We've come because the Crucifixion was real, and the verdict that we deserved was laid instead upon you. Forgive us for all the times we have looked away or remained silent. Forgive us for embracing your cross as a stunning piece of jewelry but not as a stark reminder of the inexpressible price you paid for our sake. As weak and as feeble as our faith may be, may we yet stand and keep watch with you for at least these few moments, knowing that the victory was won on that hillside long ago because of your great love. All this we would ask in your name, O Lord. Amen.

Offering Prayer (John 10)

O God, receive our tithes, our gifts, and our offerings. Although feeble compared to what you have done for us in the life and death of your Son, we pray that through the power of your Holy Spirit these gifts will be multiplied many times. We pray that your kingdom will come one step closer on this earth. Amen.

Offertory Prayer

Lord, as we give to your ministry in the world that you have given us to steward, help us gain the confidence that we who leave houses or brothers or sisters or fathers or mothers or children or fields for your name's sake, will truly inherit eternal life. Bless the giving and receiving of these our gifts, in the name of Jesus. Amen.

Offertory Prayer

Omnipotent and all-knowing God, you have given each of us so many good examples in the followers of Jesus. Those among these disciples supported the weak, fed the hungry, and clothed the naked. Even if we are not called to such rarified air, don't allow us to fail in what we can do. Remind us to not let what we cannot do interfere with what we can do as we aspire to be kingdom disciples. Amen.

Benediction

Take the yoke of the cross and turn it from a symbol of shame into a symbol of light. Jesus is the light of the world even on this Good Friday and asks us to be the lesser lights of the world. As your people, O God, make us to be a city built on a hill that cannot be concealed. Go now in power, mercy, and the strength of God, our Creator, Redeemer, and Sustainer. Amen.

Benediction

Go forth with Easter hope in your heart. As we live in the darkness of death's shadow, may we still be a people who know the light and love of Christ Jesus.

Benediction

Go with the courage of all those who have learned the truth and are willing to stand by it. Take up the cross and carry it to a world in need. And the blessing of God the Father, God the Son, and God the Holy Spirit go with you, on this day and the days to come. Amen.

Benediction

Go forth in silence, remembering God's grace poured out for you in Jesus Christ. Thanks be to God for this indescribable gift! Go into the darkness of this Good Friday evening with the light of Christ in your heart! In the name of the Father, the Son, and the Holy Spirit. Amen.

APPENDIX A: COMMUNION PRAYERS FOR LENT AND HOLY WEEK

Editor's note: the following prayers for Communion during Lent and Holy Week are to be used only in the most informal services. The prayers could serve as substitutes for the formal church liturgy as found in resources such as the *United Methodist Hymnal* (Nashville: Abingdon Press, 1989) or the United Methodist *Book of Worship*, ed. Andy Langford (Nashville: Abingdon Press, 1992). Each denomination has parallel and corresponding Communion liturgies as well. Examples in which prayers such as those found below might be best and most appropriately used would be worship occurrences, such as an informal love feast or church family campground meeting.

Prayer of Institution

On Jesus' last earthly night, as he gathered his disciples about him for a final meal together, Jesus reached out and took the bread. As he broke the loaf he prayed to God for strength, and then he offered the bread to his disciples and said the words we remember so well: "Take, eat; this is my body."

After they had eaten the bread, Jesus lifted the cup toward heaven and told the disciples as he blessed the drink: "This cup that is poured out for you is the new covenant in my blood." Tonight as we join those disciples of so long ago, we too have Jesus at the table with us. As they were persons of "clay feet," so too are we. Yet in God's infinite mercy and grace those disciples, like today's disciples, received the measure of God's grace necessary to redeem and restore them. Let us give thanks to God for God's unsearchable mercy. Amen.

Prayer of Institution

In the upper room, Jesus the Master took the loaf and blessed it. Later, Jesus took the chalice of wine and blessed it too. He told his apostles that holy night that as they ate and drank in his name, they did it as a sign of remembrance. They also ate and drank as a sign of the inbreaking of God's realm.

As we eat together, as they did on that holy evening Maundy Thursday, we eat and drink in Jesus' memory. But we also eat and drink to celebrate Jesus as the Messiah who inaugurates the kingdom of God. In this Jesus as Messiah, God has initiated a new realm. Thanks be to God. Amen.

Prayer of Institution

During what we know as the Last Supper, Jesus invited his disciples to gather about as he had a final lesson for them. Jesus lifted a loaf of bread toward the heavenly places and divided this loaf into halves. As he did, Jesus said to those gathered: "This is my body, which is given for you. Do this in remembrance of me." Just a few moments later, as the gravity of Jesus' words began to sink into the disciples' consciousness, Jesus took a goblet of wine and lifted it in prayer toward heaven. As he did, Jesus said these words: "Drink from it, all of you; for this is my blood of the covenant, which is poured out for many for the forgiveness of sins." After receiving both the loaf and goblet, the little group of devotees sang some sacred hymns and then retired to the Mount of Olives.

This night we eat, drink, and sing out of our profound thanksgiving to God for God's marvelous gift. This gift of God in the body and blood of Jesus forgives us of our sins and heals us of our infirmities. As we receive from this Lord's Table, may we be grateful disciples. Amen.

Prayer after Receiving Communion

We are thankful to you, Gracious God, for the celebrations we have just reenacted as a memorial of redemption. O Father Almighty, in this surrender of praise and prayer we have recalled not only Jesus' death on our behalf, but we also anticipate his coming in final victory. As we bring to mind Jesus' death, resurrection, and final ascension, we offer you our lives in living service in the Word. Fasten our lives in mission to your grand design for the world and make us an integral part of it. Help us incorporate that great prayer into our daily life as we join our sisters and brothers praying in unison: "Our Father, who art in heaven, hallowed be thy name. Thy kingdom come, thy will be done, on earth as it is in heaven. Give us this day our daily bread. And forgive us our trespasses, as we forgive those who trespass against us. And lead us not into temptation, but deliver us from evil. For thine is the kingdom, and the power, and the glory, forever and ever." Amen.

Prayer after Receiving Communion

Join us to the original disciples, O Lord, who as they remembered Jesus' words also came to understand his teaching and mission. Sanctify us as you did them, Eternal God. By your Holy Spirit make us be for humanity the blood and body of your anointed one. As we share the holy food and drink of Jesus, create in us a new and unending life in him. Consecrate us moreover that as we have faithfully received your sacred sacrament, we now serve you in unity, fidelity, and harmony with all humankind. At the last day bring us together with all your saints—past, present, and future—into the joy of your eternal kingdom forever and ever. Join our hearts as our voices pray together: "Our Father, who art in heaven..."

Prayer after Receiving Communion

As a congregation of the people of God we have prayed together with one unified voice the great amen of peace and mercy. Now, O Lord of this sacred meal, confirm our prayers here on earth in your heavenly realms. Make the words Jesus spoke to his disciples long ago burn in our hearts as it burned in theirs. Give us a mission and lead us to places that we can share the grace and mercy we have received at this your holy table. Seal our prayer this day with saints around the world and through the ages as we pray together: "Our Father, who art in heaven . . ."

APPENDIX B: LENTEN LECTIONARY

Readings for All Three Years

Service	Scripture Readings			
Ash Wednesday	Joel 2:1-2, 12-17	Psalm 51:1-17	2 Corinthians 5:20b–6:10	Matthew 6:1-6, 16-21
Holy Thursday	Exodus 12:1-14	Psalm 116:1-2, 12-19	1 Corinthians 11:23-26	John 13:1-17, 31b-35
Good Friday	Isaiah 52:13–53:12	Psalm 22	Hebrews 10:16-25	John 18:1–19:42

Readings for Year A

Service	Scripture Readings			
First Sunday in Lent	Genesis 2:15-17; 3:1-7	Psalm 32	Romans 5:12-19	Matthew 4:1-11
Second Sunday in Lent	Genesis 12:1-4a	Psalm 121	Romans 4:1-5, 13-17	John 3:1-17

Third Sunday in Lent	Exodus 17:1-7	Psalm 95	Romans 5:1-11	John 4:5-42
Fourth Sunday in Lent	1 Samuel 16:1-13	Psalm 23	Ephesians 5:8-14	John 9:1-41
Fifth Sunday in Lent	Ezekiel 37:1-14	Psalm 130	Romans 8:6-11	John 11:1-45
Passion/ Palm Sunday	Liturgy of the Palms			
	Matthew 21:1-11	Psalm 118:1-2, 19-29		
	Liturgy of the Passion			
	Isaiah 50:4-9a	Psalm 31:9-16	Philippians 2:5-11	Matthew 26:14–27:66; or Matthew 27:11-54

Readings for Year B

Service	Scripture Readings			
First Sunday in Lent	Genesis 9:8-17	Psalm 25:1-10	1 Peter 3:18-22	Mark 1:9-15
Second Sunday in Lent	Genesis 17:1-7, 15-16	Psalm 22:23-31	Romans 4:13-25	Mark 8:31-38
Third Sunday in Lent	Exodus 20:1-17	Psalm 19	1 Corinthians 1:18-25	John 2:13-22
Fourth Sunday in Lent	Numbers 21:4-9	Psalm 107:1-3, 17-22	Ephesians 2:1-10	John 3:14-21
Fifth Sunday in Lent	Jeremiah 31:31-34	Psalm 51:1-12	Hebrews 5:5-10	John 12:20-33
Passion/ Palm Sunday	Liturgy of the Palms			
	Mark 11:1-11	Psalm 118:1-2, 19-29		
	Liturgy of the Passion			
	Isaiah 50:4-9a	Psalm 31:9-16	Philippians 2:5-11	Mark 14:1–15:47; or Mark 15:1-39 (40-47)

Readings for Year C

Service	Scripture Readings			
First Sunday in Lent	Deuter-onomy 26:1-11	Psalm 91:1-2, 9-16	Romans 10:8b-13	Luke 4:1-13
Second Sunday in Lent	Genesis 15:1-12, 17-18	Psalm 27	Philippians 3:17–4:1	Luke 13:31-35
Third Sunday in Lent	Isaiah 55:1-9	Psalm 63:1-8	1 Corin-thians 10:1-13	Luke 13:1-9
Fourth Sunday in Lent	Joshua 5:9-12	Psalm 32	2 Corin-thians 5:16-21	Luke 15:1-3, 11b-32
Fifth Sunday in Lent	Isaiah 43:16-21	Psalm 126	Philippians 3:4b-14	John 12:1-8
Passion/ Palm Sunday	Liturgy of the Palms			
	Luke 19:28-40	Psalm 118:1-2, 19-29		
	Liturgy of the Passion			
	Isaiah 50:4-9a	Psalm 31:9-16	Philippians 2:5-11	Luke 22:14–23:56 (or Luke 23:1-49)